FREE MASK

You Will Need:

- Thin elastic, wool or string

- Scissors

- Sticky Tape

Instructions:

1. Pull out the mask page.
2. Pop out the mask.
3. Cut enough elastic/wool/string to fit around the back of your head.
4. Attach to the back of the mask with some sticky tape.
5. Have fun with your new mask!

SCISSORS ARE SHARP! ASK AN ADULT FOR HELP BEFORE USING.

Welcome

A big welcome to your amazing 1D annual!
It's packed with fun facts and fab pics. Yay!

08 Fact files Everything you need to know about the lads

20 The story so far We chart 1D's rise to the top

26 Super stats! Facts and figures on your fave boys

28 Famous fans Which celebs love the band as much as you?

30 Did you know? Funny facts about the chaps!

34 Discography How many of their songs do you own?

36 Wordsearch Find the 1D-related words in our cool quiz

38 Live! See the guys in action looking amazing on stage

40 Star style Find out the fivesome's style secrets

46 Papped! Cameras are never far away when the 1D lads are around!

48 Favourite things What do the boys love? All is revealed...

52 Quiz: Who said what? Match the quotes to the band members

54 Famous friends The lads have plenty of celeb pals

56 Quiz: Spot the difference Can you spot the 5 differences?

60 Why we love 1D Where do we start?!

64 The giant 1D quiz Test your knowlededge of the great group

70 Tweet tweet! The boys best tweets. Lol!

72 I love 1D because... Write down your top reasons here!

74 Quiz: Guess the body parts Can you tell who's who?

76 Quiz answers How many have you got right?

Published 2013.

Pedigree Books Limited, Beech Hill House,
Walnut Gardens, Exeter, Devon EX4 4DH

www.pedigreebooks.com | books@pedigreegroup.co.uk

ISBN 9781907602894

Fantastic facts
LOUIS

Louis, AKA Lou Bou Bear, hates beans, loves parties

Full name Louis William Tomlinson

DOB 24th December, 1991

From Doncaster

Nickname Lou Boo Bear

Height 5-feet 9-inches

Siblings Four sisters, Twins Daisy and Phoebe, Charlotte and Felicite

Likes Macaroni cheese, cookie dough, partying

Dislikes Smoking, baked beans and not getting enough sleep

Favourite song Look After You by The Fray

Superpower he would most like To be able to stay young forever

Before 1D Louis was at college and working in a cinema

Top grooming product Dry shampoo, as he doesn't enjoy washing his hair very much

Fave aftershave Hollister

Sleeping attire Pyjama bottoms or nothing

Random! Louis likes putting on silly voices, and is very good at them

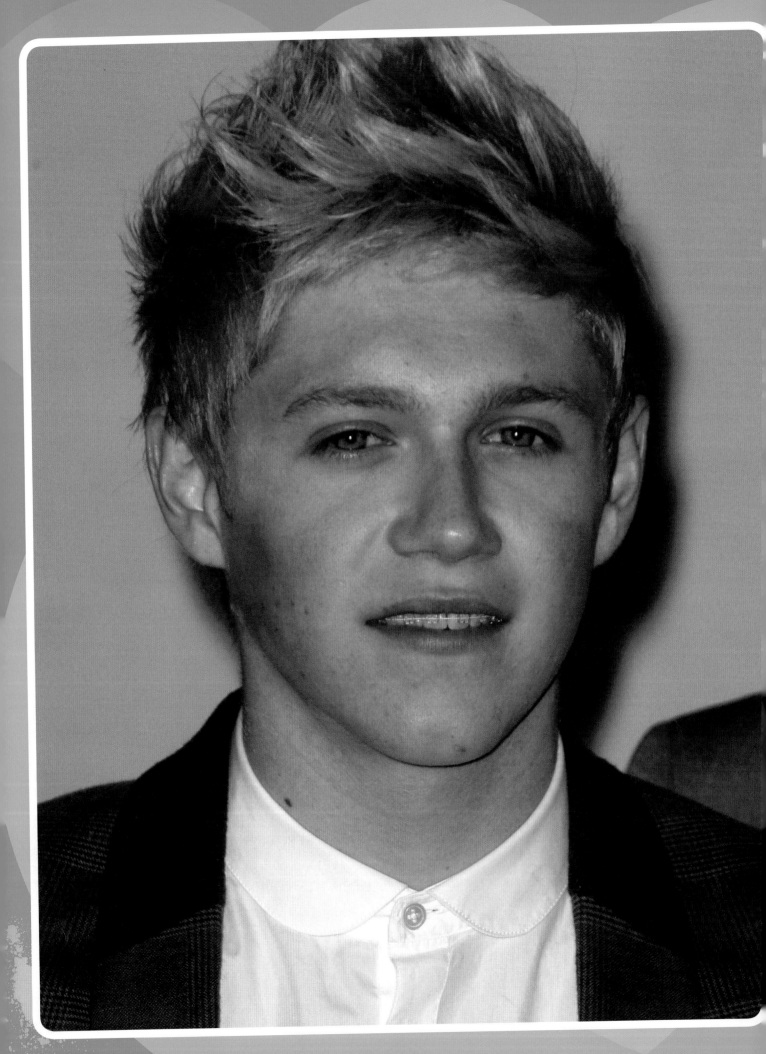

Fantastic facts
NIALL

The Irish lad is cheeky, charming and likes parping!

Full name Niall James Horan

DOB 13th September, 1993

From: Mullingar, Ireland

Nickname Nialler

Height: 5-feet 7-inches

Siblings One older brother, Greg

Likes Giraffes, Michael Bublé, passing wind!

Dislikes Being hungry, clowns, dodgy chat up lines

Favourite song Fly Me To The Moon by Frank Sinatra

First ever concert Busted

Superpower he would most like He would love to be completely invisible

Before 1D Niall was planning to go to uni and study civil engineering.

Top grooming product L'Oréal products to keep his amazing quiff in shape

Fave aftershave Mania by Armani

Sleeping attire Just his pants

Random! Niall would like to be able to hug every single one of the band's fans. Ahhhh!

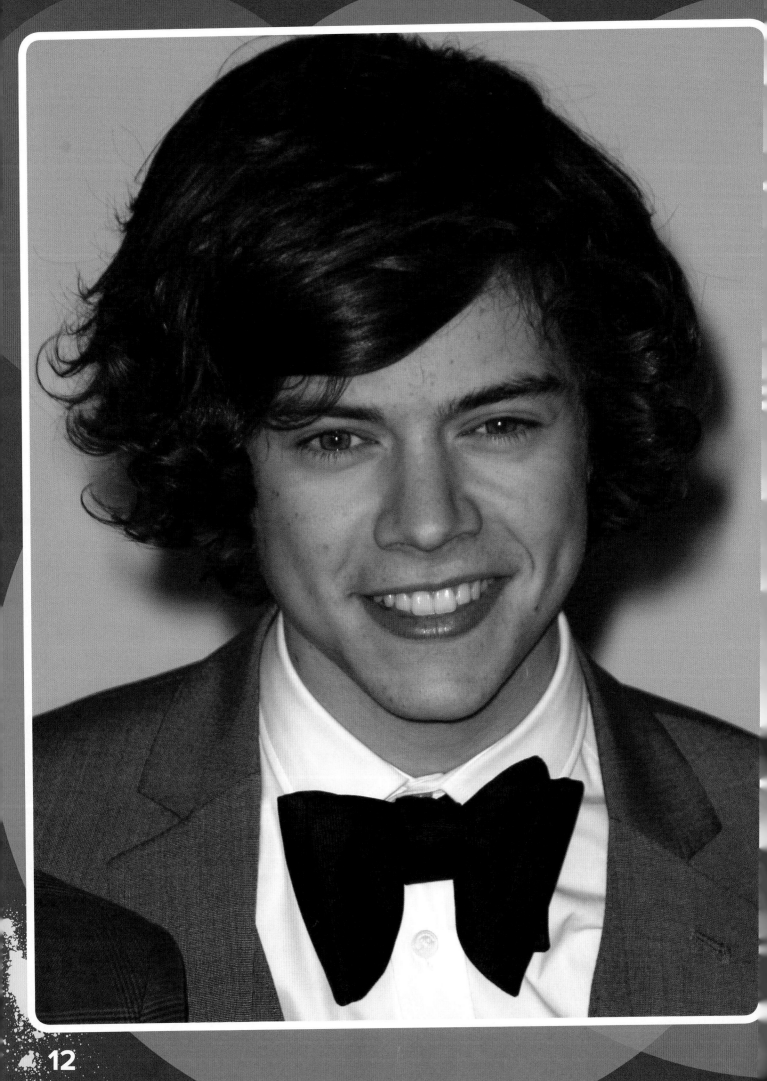

Fantastic facts
HARRY

Harry likes tacos, Adele and sleeps in his birthday suit

Full name Harry Edward Styles

DOB 1st February, 1994

From Cheshire

Nickname Hazza

Height 5-feet 10-inches

Siblings One older sister, Gemma

Likes Tacos, Adele, Man United

Dislikes Olives, swearing and people being rude

Favourite song Shine On You Crazy Diamond by Pink Floyd

First ever concert Nickelback

Superpower he would most like Time travel

Before 1D Harry had a part time job in a bakery

Top grooming product L'Oréal Elvive shampoo to keep his curls bouncy!

Fave aftershave Diesel Fuel For Life

Sleeping attire Nothing at all!

Random! Harry cuddles a pillow when he's trying to get to sleep

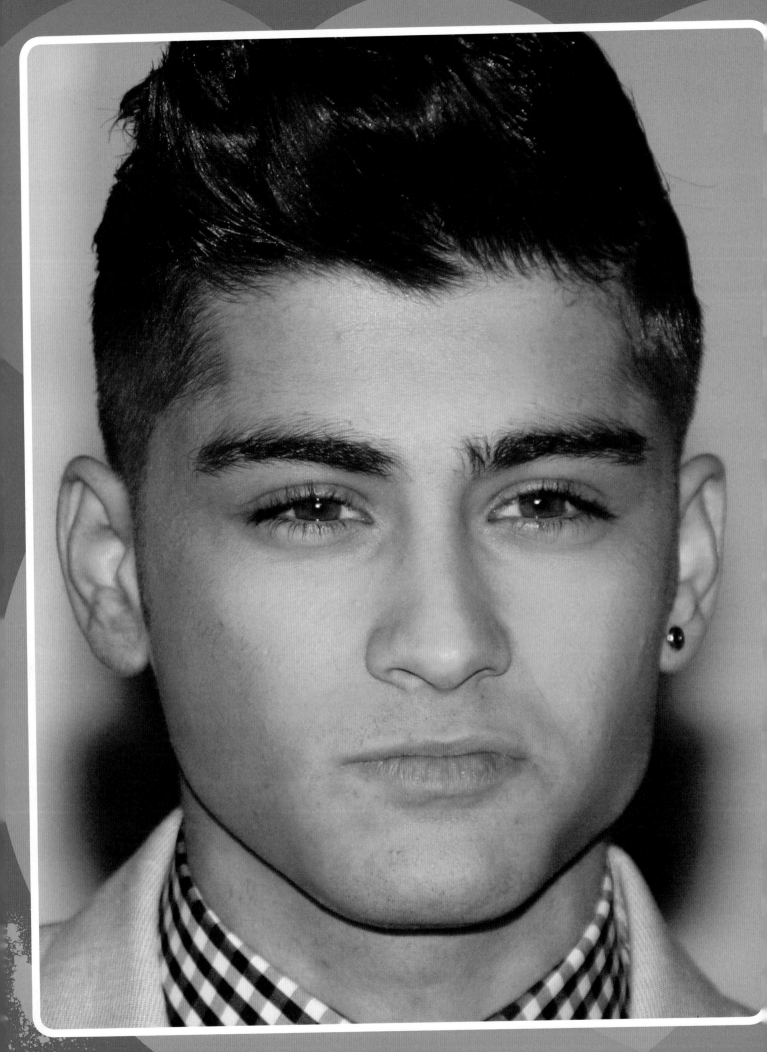

Fantastic facts
ZAYN

He wishes he could fly and is a fan of Family Guy

Full name Zayn Jawaad Malik

DOB 12th January, 1993

From Bradford

Nickname: Zaynster

Height 5-feet 9-inches

Siblings: Three sisters, Doniya, Waliyha, Safaa

Likes Tattoos (not v surprising!), Chris Brown and Family Guy

Dislikes Pyjamas, sandwich crusts, swimming pools

Favourite song Thriller by Michael Jackson

First ever concert JLS

Superpower he would most like Being able to fly

Before 1D Zayn planned to become a drama teacher

Top grooming product Any kind of hair wax

Fave aftershave Unforgivable by Sean John

Sleeping attire Zero!

Random! Zayn's favourite body part is his jawline

Fantastic facts
LIAM

Want all the facts about Liam? They're all yours!

Full name Liam James Payne

DOB 29th August, 1993

From Wolverhampton

Nickname Paynee

Height 5-feet 10-inches

Siblings Two sisters, Nicole and Ruth

Likes Chocolate, basketball and singing in the shower

Dislikes Mean tweets, spoons and flying

Favourite song Happy Birthday

First ever concert Gareth Gates

Superpower he would most like To be invisible

Before 1D Liam was singing loads and also studying for his A-levels

Top grooming product A good strong hair wax

Fave aftershave 1 Million by Paco Rabanne

Sleeping attire Nothing!

Random! Liam is hugely romantic and likes buying girls flowers

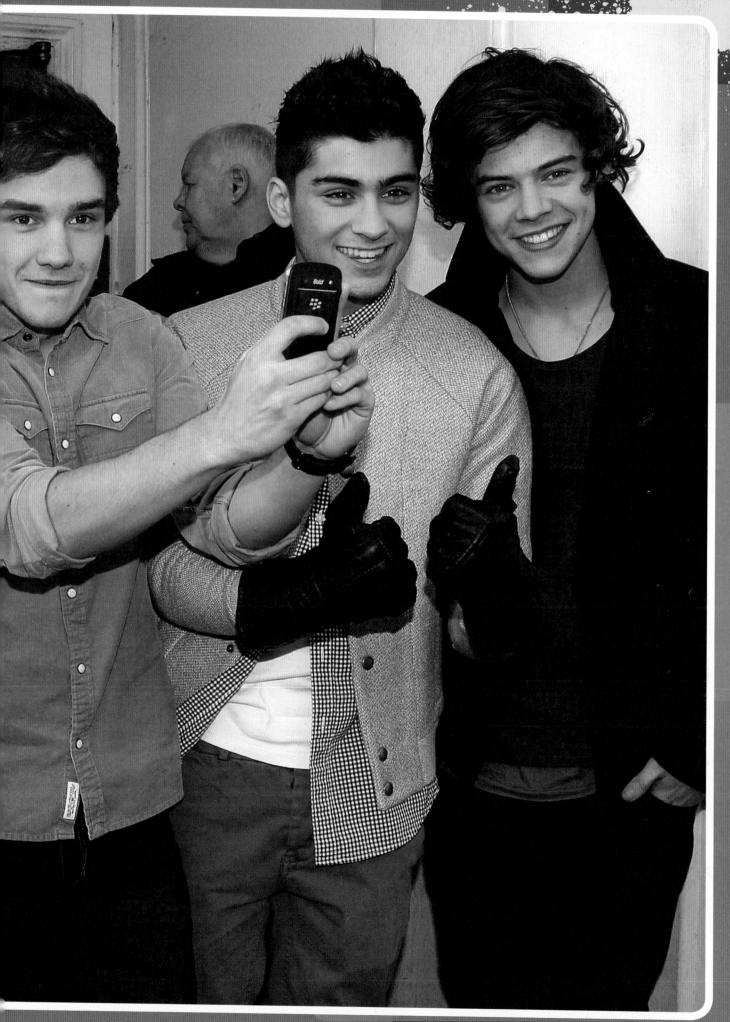

It's a One Direction denim frenzy!

1D: Offically huge

The story so far

They're the biggest band in the world and we love everything about them. How did it all go so right...

Back in 2010, five normal boys were dreaming of pop stardom. And where better place to showcase their singing talents than on the mighty X Factor? Liam, Louis, Niall, Zayn and Harry all went along to try their luck as solo singers that spring. But during the Bootcamp stage, the judges decided that although they were brilliant performers individually, they would be even more amazing as a band. They all jumped at the chance to try out as a five-piece at Judges' Houses, and started rehearsing straight away.

They had just six weeks to get to know each other and polish their routine, so they all headed to Harry's house in Cheshire and practiced non-stop to make sure they were ready to take on the other acts in Marbella.

When Judges' Houses rolled around and it was time to showcase their talents for Simon Cowell, the guys chose to sing Natalia Imbruglia's classic single Torn, and they were swiftly chosen as one of Simon's four acts for the live shows. They were one step closer to winning the £1million record contact.

The boys were aiming for the top from the start

From Day One the audience and judges loved the lads and their feedback got better week after week. They were hotly tipped to win, but during the final they were pipped to the post by Matt Cardle and Rebecca Ferguson, who came first and second respectively.

But all was not lost! They were offered a lucrative record deal by Simon Cowell's record label Syco, and within weeks they jetted to LA and Sweden to work with some of the industry's most respected producers.

Their first single, the anthemic What Makes You Beautiful, was released in September 2011. It provided them with their first Number One and cemented their status at the UK's most exciting new band.

The ballad Gotta Be You followed next, and their debut album, Up All Night, was released later that month. Their third single release, One Thing, was unleashed onto the UK public in January 2012, and soon afterwards, the lads headed to Australia and America on their very first international promo tour.

The rest of the world soon fell in love with the fivesome, and before you could say, 'Take Me Home' they had

The lads have millions of dedicated fans all over the world

recorded and released their second album, which went to Number One across the globe.

In 2013, the boys embarked on an eight-month sold-out world tour, and also filmed their very first movie, This Is Us, which took fans behind the scenes of 1D's world. They're currently working on their third album [scream!] and things are getting bigger and better for the guys all the time. We can't wait to see what the future brings!

Louis: A bit excited about winning a BRIT

1D

One Direction in numbers

Number of BRIT Awards won **2**

Number of waxwork figures made by Madame Tussauds **5**

Number of countries Up All Night went to Number One **16**

Tickets sold per minute for their 2013 world tour:
1000

Number of copies of Up All Night sold worldwide:
Over 3 million

Number of minutes their 2012 Australian tour sold out in **3**

Number of Facebook fans
14.5 million

Number of copies of What Makes You Beautiful sold worldwide Over
5 million

Number of Twitter followers Harry has
12 million

Number of countries Take Me Home has gone to Number One in:
36

Up All Night – The Live Tour DVD hit Number One in **27** countries

Vevo views of What Makes You Beautiful
Over 100 million

Number of Twitter followers 1D have:
Over 11 million

YouTube views: 490 million

Famous fans

It's not just us who thinks 1D are the universe, this bunch of famous faces love them too!

Katy Perry

Superstar Katy loves the lads and when they scored their first Number One, she tweeted: "Congratulations, you didn't let me down! xo."

Joe Jonas

Joe knows a thing or two about being a pop star. He reckons the lads are ace and has said of them, "They are top boys. I love their songs."

Demi Lovato

The guys met Demi on the US X Factor. It was rumoured that she dated Niall, but it was nothing more than gossip. Phew.

Selena Gomez

Justin Bieber's ex has admitted she rates the boys and was seen singing along when they performed at the Kids' Choice Awards.

Kendall Jenner

The cute Kardashian adores the boys and has been to see them in concert. She even made her very own 1D banner.

Nicole Scherzinger

Nicole was one of the judges who put 1D together on The X Factor, and she's still one of their biggest supporters to this day.

Did you know?

⭐ Harry once spent thousands of pounds on pizza, then drove around LA handing them out to homeless people. Awwwww!

⭐ Louis has appeared in TV shows Waterloo Road and Fat Friends and would love to do more acting in the future.

Don't ever expect Niall to share food!

⭐ Harry was attacked by a goat when he was 10 years old!

⭐ If Liam had to be a fruit he would be a banana!

⭐ What Makes You Beautiful was the fastest selling song of 2011.

⭐ Niall supported fellow former X Factor contestant Lloyd Daniels at his sell-out gig in Dublin's O2 Theatre in 2009.

⭐ Zayn had his first kiss with a girl when he was 10. She was taller than him so he stood on a brick to reach her!

⭐ Niall's pet hate is people taking food off of his plate.

Liam does his best banana impression

★ All of the boys had to change their mobile numbers after they got leaked on the internet.

★ Zayn's ideal date with a girl would be chilling out on a sofa watching films and talking.

★ Harry's hair was straight when he was younger!

★ Louis has always wanted a little brother and he can't wait to have a son of his own.

★ Niall used to have two fish called Tom and Jerry, but they died because he overfed them.

★ Liam calls himself Batman and Niall Fartman!

★ Zayn can't swim and he has a fear of open water.

★ Harry said he found signing his very first autograph weird because until then he didn't have a signature. He ended up simply writing 'Harry'.

★ They call Simon Cowell 'Uncle Simon' and admit that they're very cheeky to him.

★ The band's debut UK tour sold out within 12 minutes!

1D

Discography

Singles

Heroes
(with the X Factor finalists)
November 2010 (Number 1)

What Makes You Beautiful
September 2011 (Number 1)

Gotta Be You
November 2011 (Number 3)

Wishing On A Star
(with The X Factor contestants)
November 2011 (Number 1)

One Thing
January 2012 (Number 9)

More Than This
May 2012 (Number 86)

Live While We're Young
September 2012 (Number 3)

Little Things
November 2012 (Number 1)

Kiss You
February 2013 (Number 9)

One Way or Another
(Teenage Kicks)
February 2013 (Number 1)

Albums

Up All Night
November 2011 (Number 2)

Take Me Home
November 2012 (Number 1)

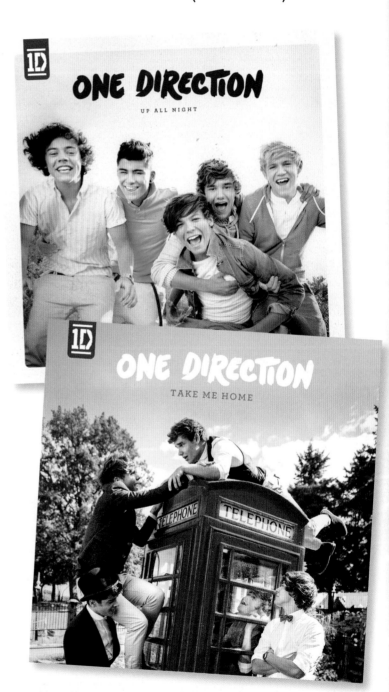

Harry will always be our Number 1

Wordsearch

Can you find all of the 1D related words in our puzzle?

N	V	H	G	V	B	E	R	Z	U	J	D	T	A	B
Y	O	Y	A	A	V	O	R	P	S	E	O	R	E	H
A	Z	D	N	R	T	Y	A	M	A	Z	I	N	G	L
U	O	D	N	C	R	L	A	I	M	B	T	X	T	L
E	Q	Z	A	O	L	Y	U	L	O	M	A	I	O	A
D	N	F	H	N	L	E	U	I	M	P	K	P	U	I
K	X	O	I	L	U	F	I	T	U	A	E	B	R	N
U	I	G	R	C	B	G	T	T	P	P	M	A	I	L
U	H	S	W	E	T	G	W	L	O	D	E	A	X	Y
T	O	R	S	H	B	W	K	E	M	L	H	C	H	I
F	V	Q	I	Y	Z	M	S	K	Y	K	O	I	J	J
F	U	N	N	Y	O	I	U	X	G	F	M	R	H	G
C	G	D	N	B	U	U	U	N	E	F	E	E	R	V
S	L	J	K	O	I	D	U	U	J	R	P	M	Q	L
C	U	Y	L	E	Y	D	J	O	B	L	T	A	X	W

- ★ Amazing
- ★ America
- ★ Band
- ★ Beautiful
- ★ Funny
- ★ Harry
- ★ Heroes
- ★ Kissyou
- ★ Liam
- ★ Little
- ★ London
- ★ Louis
- ★ Niall
- ★ Numberone
- ★ Takemehome
- ★ Things
- ★ Tour
- ★ Upallnight
- ★ Xfactor

Harry's hidden somewhere in the worldsearch!

Live!

The lads love getting up on stage, and we love watching them!

Louis: "Mum, is that you over there?"

Harry's waxwork was shockingly realistic

The boys were oblivious to the phone box pile up

Zayn won the game of musical statues

Niall: "The words will come back to me any minute now."

Super Stylin'

Checked shirt

Hoody

Trainers

1D manage to look good in whatever they wear, but how do they make their style work...

Shopping style

1D always look cool. When it comes to favourite brands the lads love Bench, Caterpillar, G Star and Superdry, and they also like shopping at TopMan and ASOS. The lucky lads get gifted togs from various brands, and they also buy the odd designer pieces to mix in with their high street buys.

Checked shirts

Thanks to their love of checked shirts, the fivesome could share a wardrobe if they needed to. They must have quite a collection between them!

Shades

The boys are rarely seen without a trusty pair of shades, and they've all sported a pair of cool Ray-Bans at different times.

Toms

Louis helped make Toms a must-have shoe, and although he's decided it's a bit silly to wear them without socks in the winter, as soon as the summer comes he digs them out!

Trainers

Niall is the biggest trainer wearer of the group. His favourites are Fred Perry tennis trainers and Nike Dunks, which have a retro twist.

Hoodies

You can always tell when one of the 1D crew are tired, because they'll be rocking a comfy hoodie. They like oversized Jack Wills numbers.

Sharp suits

The band have smartened up since the early days, and although they still love their laid-back gear, they're often suited and booted for awards events.

Suits

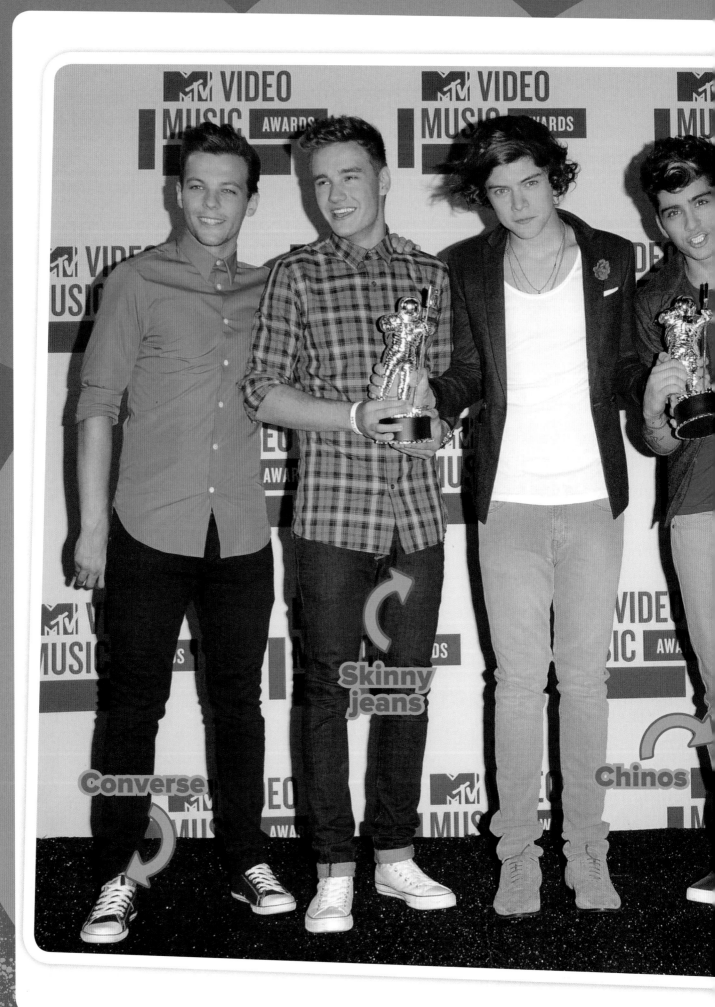

Converse

The fivesome are often seen in cool Converse. A fan even customised a pair especially for Niall, writing, 'marry me Niall Horan', on the side.

Caps

Liam and Nialll have been spotted wearing caps, which are the perfect way to hide a bad hair day! Not that they ever have any, obvs...

Skinny jeans

All of the boys rock skinny jeans, apart from Niall who prefers the baggy look.

Onesies

The band first rocked onesises back in the early X Factor days, and although they're no longer seen out in them, they do secretly cosy up in them behind the scenes.

Chinos

If they ever get bored with jeans, chinos are always the lads' number one back up.

Stripes

Louis seems to have calmed down his stripe-wearing these days, but he still manages to sneak them into his outfits sometimes...

Lovely Lou

The band's amazing stylist, Lou Teasdale, ensures that the guys always look coordinated and very slick.

Past disasters

They may look super-cool, but Harry says he's embarrassed when he looks back at some of The X Factor clothes. He reckons there's "no excuse!" for some of the outfits. Lol.

Papped!

No matter where they go, there is no escape from the paps!

Fan: "Look what I had for dinner last night, Harry!"

That's a funny shaped suitcase Niall

Pop star in dragging his own case - shocker!

Liam: "Come any closer with that camera and I'll squirt you!"

Zayn was temporarily blinded by the world's shiniest jacket

A few of their favourite

They're our fave thing, but what do the boys love?

Curly hair
Hazza reckons he'd cry if anyone tried to straighten his locks! We think we would, too...

Robbie Williams
All of the guys are mates with him and Louis says he was his 'inspiration'.

I'm Sexy And I Know It by LMFAO
Liam admits it's the song he plays over and over on his iPod.

Drawing
Zayn draws in any spare moments he has, and would love to put on his own art show one day.

Moments
The Ed Sheeran-penned track is Louis' favourite.

The fans!
Say no more. The boys think their fans are the best in the universe.

Nando's
Liam reckons their chicken is the best in the world, and the group often get take outs when they're on shoots.

things...

Cheryl Cole

All of the boys have a crush on the former X Factor judge.

Each other

Zayn says that they're closer now than they've ever been.

Screaming!

Niall says he loves hearing the fans screaming, because it shows that they're having a good time.

Instruments

All of the guys are keen to learn more instruments and plan to make their third album more 'live' sounding.

Tattoos

All the guys apart from Niall have got loads.

Michael Bublé

The crooner has become top pals with the band. Niall's over the moon because he has been a fan of Mr Bublé for years.

Who said what?

1 My trademark saying is probably "VAS HAPPENIN?!"

2 "If it were legal, I'd marry food."

3 "Feel free to insult me, but you don't have the right to insult our fans."

4 "If a man whistles at you, don't turn around, ignore him. You're a lady, not a dog."

5 "The strongest people aren't always the people who win, but the people who don't give up when they lose."

6 "Who doesn't need an eraser? Everyone makes mistakes."

7 "Life is hard, but if it weren't, where would the challenge be?"

8 "Just because you don't have a prince, doesn't mean you're not a princess."

9 "A real girl isn't perfect, and a perfect girl isn't real."

10 "We're not perfect, we're not clean cut. We're trying to be ourselves."

11 "I wish I had a girl to cuddle up to at night rather than my pillow."

12 "I was gonna say 'great', but then I said 'good', so I say 'groot'."

13 "I've always preferred having girlfriends to just seeing people."

14 "My accent always works with girls. They like it. I have no idea why."

15 "A smile could last for a second but the memory of it could last for a lifetime."

Zayn was upset when
Niall stole the mic

Showbiz pals

Liam and co have got more famous friends than you can shake a stick at!

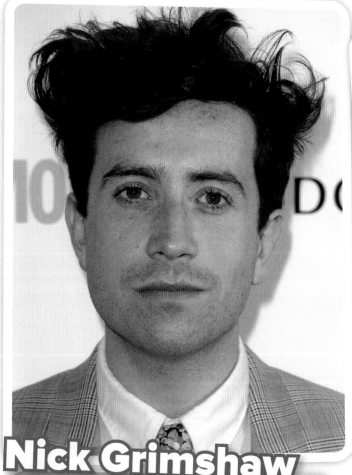

Nick Grimshaw

The Radio 1 DJ has been friends with the boys since the early days, and he and Harry often hang out at swanky parties together.

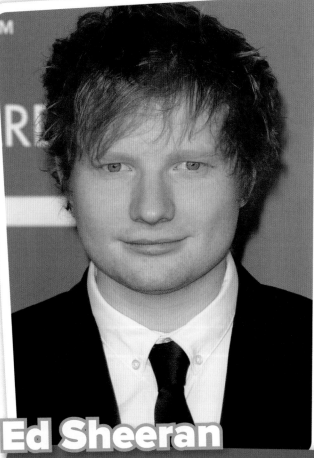

Ed Sheeran

The talented chap is really close to all of the guys and has written several songs for them, including the amazing Little Things.

Little Mix

The guys met Little Mix during The X Factor, and now Zayn and Perrie are going out together, the two groups are closer than ever.

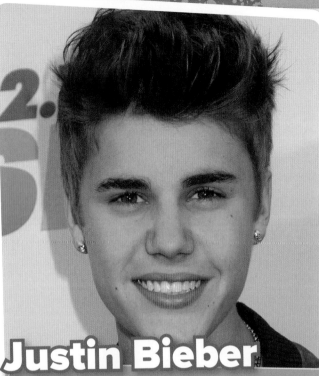

2.

Justin Bieber

All of the guys were fans of Justin before they met him, and as soon as they were introduced they got on brilliantly. Jealous? Us?

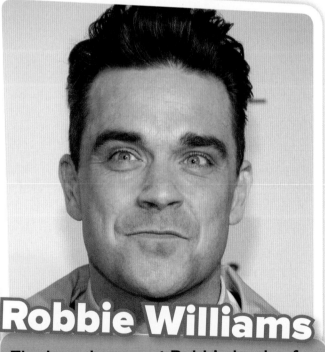

Robbie Williams

The boys have met Robbie loads of times, and the former Take That-er has given them some great advice about being in a boy band. He certainly knows a thing or two!

James Corden

James and Louis first met on the set of TV show Fat Friends many years ago. The hilarious actor and presenter has since become friendly with all of the group.

Spot the difference

See if you can spot the five funny differences between these two pics of the 1D lads!

Answers on page 76

Why we love 1D

We could write a hundred books on why we love 1D

Here are some of the top reasons!

They like girls who dress down

"I really love it when girls wear a dress and Converse. That is so hot, when she's just casual," says Harry.

They're charitable

The guys released a single, One Way Or Another (Teenage Kicks), in aid of Comic Relief, and scored a massive Number One, raising loads of money for the charity. They also visited Ghana to raise awareness of the poverty there.

They don't care what other people think

"I like the term misunderstood. But I am a bit of a bad boy. I have tattoos and I mess around. That's part of my image, so it's cool," Zayn says.

They're romantic

Harry says, "When it comes to the perfect date, I'm quite old-fashioned. I like going out to dinner. You have the chance to talk to somebody and get to know them better."

They're down to earth

All they ask for backstage at gigs is water and tea. They say they'd laugh if anyone turned into a diva!

The boys always make time for their fans

Zayn likes being a bad boy

Hands up if you love 1D!

Harry: "Yes, that's two pizzas please."

Having a bad hair day, Niall?

They're, er, sweet!

Their pre-stage ritual involves eating Haribo and having food fights, but they always clean up after themselves.

They still get starstruck

Niall admits that he screamed when Justin Bieber started following him on Twitter, and they still get excited when they see big name celebs at premieres and parties.

They love messing around

If Louis is bored he likes to poke Harry to annoy him, and all of the lads enjoy winding each other up and play fighting. Er, can we join in?!

They love a laugh

As Zayn says: "Once I shaved off Louis' eyebrows and then Louis shaved off Liam's and then Harry shaved his initials into the hairs on my leg while I was asleep."

They can stand up for themselves

When singer Jake Bugg took the mickey out of them, feisty Louis Tweeted: "Hi @ JakeBugg do you think slagging off boy bands makes you more indie?"

They're generous

The boys love treating their friends and family now they've got some money in the bank. Liam says it's the best thing about earning lots of dosh. Awww!

The GIANT 1D Quiz

How much do you know about 1D?

We challenge you to try our top quiz and find out!

1 What is Louis' middle name?

2 What was the name of the band's first ever single release as a band?

3 What was the first concert Niall ever went to?

4 Where does Harry come from?

5 What is Zayn's favourite song of all time?

6 How many sisters does Louis have?

7 Which superpower would Liam like to have?

8 Which angst-ridden song did the boys perform at Judges' Houses?

9 Which 1D-er had to stand on a brick when he had his first snog, because the girl in question was taller than him?

10 Where is Liam from?

11 What is Niall's middle name?

12 What is Harry's sister's name?

13 Who hates people nicking his food?

14 What is Louis' nickname?

15 Complete the title of this 1D single: Little ******

Q5

Q16

16 What kind of shop did Harry work in before the band?

17 What is 1D's second album called?

18 What is the band's stylist called?

19 How many BRIT awards have 1D won?

20 What is Liam's nickname for Niall?

21 Which judge was the group's mentor on The X Factor?

Q19

Q22

22 Which band member once drove around LA giving out free pizza to homeless people?

23 Which sweets do they request backstage at gigs?

24 What was the first concert Liam ever went to?

25 Who was attacked by a goat when they were young?

26 How long did it take for their debut tour to sell out?

Q25

27 How many sisters does Zayn have?

28 What was the name of the single the lads recorded with their fellow X Factor contestants?

29 Who is Niall's all time fave male singer?

30 Who once appeared in the TV show Fat Friends?

Answers on page76

1D

Tweet twoo!

One Direction make us #ROFL and #lovethemevenmore with their tweets!

@Real_Liam_Payne
"I just had monster munch and 2 milky bars for breakfast"

@Louis_Tomlinson
"I must say I never ever get burnt but today I look like Paul Scholes stranded in the desert ..."

@zaynmalik
"I can't get over you guys. Don't get how much you amaze me. Thank you for everything, you truly are the best fans in the world. Love you all x"

@Real_Liam_Payne
"Thanks to fudge for all the hair products to go on tour with now I've finally got my hair back ;)"

@Louis_Tomlinson
"The biggest thank you possible in 140 characters to everyone worldwide who has bought our album and single. You inspire us!"

@NiallOfficial
"Got me bus slippers on! the driver got them for us as a present!"

@Louis_Tomlinson
"We're in a position that others dream of. We love you guys. You put us here! Don't think it's forgotten."

@NiallOfficial
"Havin an 80's music night tonight! The production on All Night Long by Lionel Richie is amazing! Years ahead of itself."

@Real_Liam_Payne
"Everybody meet mine and @daniellepeazer new dog Loki :)"

@Harry_Styles
"The amount of time you guys put in to doing things for us is amazing. So again, thank you for everything you've done. It feels nice, love. x"

@zaynmalik
"We wouldn't be where we are now without you all! So Happy 2013! Love you all! :) x"

@Harry_Styles
"Just had my first ice bath. Note: If someone is laughing as you're getting into something, you probably should stop getting in."

@NiallOfficial
"Morning! This is it ! I'm goin to the dentist! I think this is my last hour with braces! Oh how I'm gona miss them! Naaaaaaat!"

@Louis_Tomlinson
"Feeling my old punk days listening to Green Day!"

@zaynmalik
"You said you know my heart is good, but you would hate me if you could, if I would allow you to, you would... X"

I love 1D because...

There are a million and one things to love about 1D.

Write down your fave reasons, right here...

I loved it when they...

My favourite 1D single is...

I think they are really talented because...

I first started liking them when...

They are my favourite band because...

My favourite band member is   because...

I will never forget when they...

....

....

They make me laugh so much when...

....

....

If I could give 1D any present it would be...

....

....

If I went out on a date with 1D I would want to go to...

....

....

When I listen to 1D's music it makes me feel...

....

....

I can do a great dance routine to...

....

....

If I met 1D I would...

....

....

My favourite 1D merchandise is...

....

....

If 1D came to my house I would...

....

....

Body talk

Can you guess who's who from the body parts we've zoomed in on in our crazy quiz?

1

2

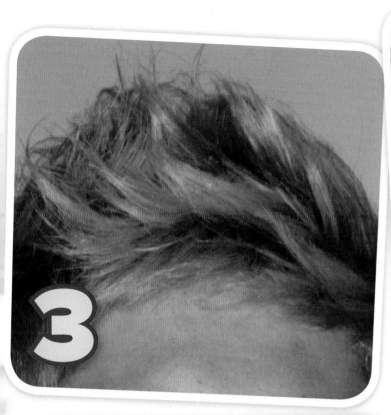

Answers

The Big Quiz

1 William

2 What Makes You Beautiful

3 Busted

4 Cheshire

5 Thriller by Michael Jackson

6 Four

7 To be invisible

8 Natalie Imbruglia's Torn

9 Harry

10 Wolverhampton

11 James

12 Jemma

13 Niall

14 Lou Bou Bear

15 Things

16 A bakery

17 Take Me Home

18 Lou Teasdale

19 Two

20 Fartman

21 Simon Cowell

22 Zayn

23 Haribo

24 Gareth Gates

25 Harry

26 12 minutes

27 Three

28 Heroes

29 Michael Buble

30 Louis

Body talk

1 Harry

2 Louis

3 Niall

4 Liam

5 Louis

6 Niall

Who said what

1 Zayn

2 Louis

3 Niall

4 Liam

5 Louis

6 Harry

7 Zayn

8 Zayn

9 Louis

10 Niall

11 Zayn

12 Liam

13 Niall

14 Harry

15 Liam

Spot the difference

1 The spots behind the boys are different colours

2 Liam's wearing a cool Union Jack wristband on his right hand

3 The spots have vanished from Louis' shirt

4 Zayn's wearing a flower just like Harry's

5 One of Liam's collars has magically changed colour from white to green

Wordsearch

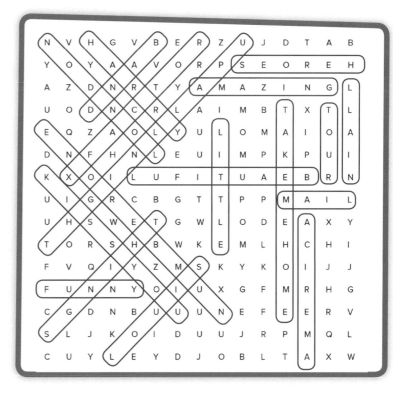

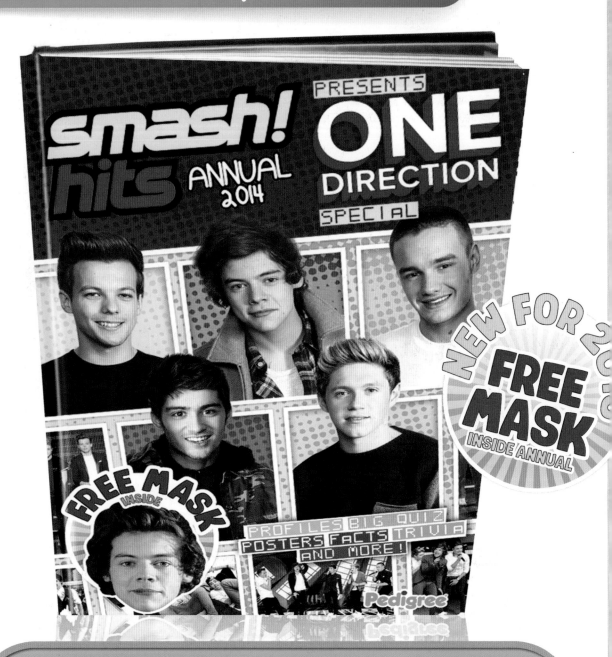